South Florida (fresh and salt water)

North and Central American desert water habitats (fresh water)

Brazilian coastal rain forest (fresh water)

ENDANGERED WATER HABITATS

The places listed here are only some of the most endangered habitats (living spaces) for salt and freshwater fishes around the world. Acid rain, pollution, real estate development, and misuse by humans are reasons these areas are threatened. All of these habitats contain fishes that are rare and can be found only here.

WHAT
IS A
FISH
?

BARBARA R. STRATTON

A New England Aquarium Book

FRANKLIN WATTS
New York • London • Toronto • Sydney
1991

Front cover: This view of a French angelfish focuses on the most important feature that makes it a fish—the gill cover and the gills behind it, which enable fishes to remove life-giving oxygen from the surrounding water.

Frontispiece: This bottom-dwelling fish called the diamond blenny uses its fins to perch in the tentacles of a flowery sea animal called an anemone.

To Jim, who has always loved the water,
and to Paco, who hates to get his feet wet

ACKNOWLEDGMENTS

I thank everyone at the New England Aquarium who helped with this project, especially Ken Mallory, who had the enthusiasm, persistence, and patience to pull it all together. I also thank those who helped me learn to see nature in a special way: my family, my former colleagues at *Ranger Rick's Nature Magazine*, and the authors and artists I have been fortunate to work with over the years, especially Roger Tory Peterson. Elaine Bazarian, Don Curiale, Joan Downing, Mary Norris, Joseph Veneziano, and Jim Stratton gave me their personal support when I needed it most.

Photographs copyright © : Fred Bavendam: pp. 1, 5 top, 6 top right, 6 center left, 6 bottom left, 7, 11, 12, 14, 21, 23; Animals Animals: pp. 3 (Richard Kolar), 5 bottom (Steve Earley), 13 bottom (Miriam Austerman), 15, 17 (both G.I. Bernard/OSF), 16, 24 (both Breck P. Kent), 26 right (Juan M. Renjifo), 28 left (Mickey Gibson), 29 (Zig Leszczynski); Andrew Martinez: pp. 4 top, 6 top left, 6 bottom right, 9, 19; Marty Snyderman: p. 4 bottom; New England Aquarium: pp. 6 center right, 8, 10, 13 top (all Paul Erickson), 18, 27 (both Scott Kraus), 22 (Ken Mallory), 28 right (Mike DeMocker); Loren McIntyre: p. 26 left.

Library of Congress Cataloging-in-Publication Data

Stratton, Barbara R.
    What is a fish? / by Barbara R. Stratton.
      p. cm.
    "A New England Aquarium book."
    Includes bibliographical references.
    Summary: Examines the common characteristics of fishes and describes different types, including the eel and shark.
    ISBN 0-531-15223-5. — ISBN 0-531-11020-6 (lib.bdg.)
    1. Fishes—Juvenile literature. [1. Fishes.] I. Title.
QL617.2.S76   1991
597—dc20   91-18505 CIP AC

A fish is an animal that lives and swims in the water. Instead of arms, wings, or legs, a fish has fins and a tail. Using its fins and tail, a fish moves easily through the water. Water glides smoothly over a fish's body, which is covered with scales and a slimy, protective coating. A fish's body is supported by a backbone.

A fish has no hair or fur. It does not need to keep warm. Wherever a fish lives, its body takes on the temperature of the water around it.

▼ The goldfish has fins which are typical of many fishes. Two sets of paired fins, one set along its belly and the other along its sides, work like the flaps of an airplane to help steer the fish. The tail fin pushes the fish forward. The two trailing fins on the fish's back and stomach act like a ship's keel. Inside the fish, below its backbone, is an organ called the swim bladder (not seen in photo), which the fish can inflate and deflate like a balloon to rise or sink in the water.

swim bladder (not visible in photo)   top fin   scales

tail   bottom fin   paired fins   gill opening   gill cover

There are more than thirty thousand kinds of fishes in the world. They come in many sizes and shapes. A dwarf goby from the Philippines is less than one-quarter of an inch (6 mm) long when fully grown. Others, such as the whale shark or oarfish, can reach a length of over 35 feet (about 11 m). How would you like to meet a fish that is as long as two school buses, parked end to end?

▶ Some gobies are among the smallest fishes in the ocean. This shark-nose goby grows no more than a few inches in length. It is sitting among the volcano-like houses of tiny animals called corals.

▼ The world's largest fish, the whale shark, can reach the length of two school buses parked end to end.

▲ When threatened by another animal, the porcupinefish swallows water to make its pincushion spines erect. Once the porcupinefish has been inflated, few fishes care to take a bite.

◄ The pointed, arrow shape of mackerel helps them to swim in quick bursts of speed to capture their favorite food—small invertebrates and baby fishes.

The shape of a fish's body is often a good clue to the kind of place where it lives and how it finds its food. Fishes that swim fast, like tuna and mackerel, have long, tapered bodies that are shaped rather like a cigar or a torpedo. These fishes can move quickly through the ocean to find and pursue their prey. Their prey—the animals they catch and eat—is usually a school of smaller fishes.

Some fishes are shaped like a box or a balloon. These fishes cannot swim very fast, but it is hard for other fishes to swallow them. A porcupinefish that has blown itself up makes a very large and prickly mouthful.

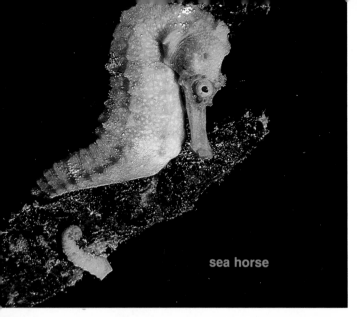

sea horse

mosshead warbonnet

torpedo ray

anemonefish

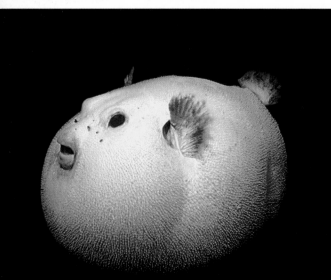

pufferfish

frogfish

Other fishes, like angelfish and butterfly fish, have bodies with nearly flat sides. These fishes are brightly colored, but their narrow bodies make it easy for them to hide or dart through openings in a coral reef. Most predators—animals that hunt other animals—are too big to follow them through these escape hatches.

Banded butterfly fish have thin, flat bodies that make it more difficult for other fishes to see them head-on. Their shape also helps them to fit into hiding places on a coral reef.

Many fishes that live on or near the bottom of the ocean, lakes, ponds, or rivers have bodies that are almost flat on top or the bottom, or both. It is hard to spot a stingray or a flounder lying on the bottom of the ocean, both because of its shape and because its colors match the sand. A hungry predator will often swim right by. Unsuspecting prey can also be easily confused. And by the time a potential meal recognizes there is a fish hidden in the sand, it is usually too late. GULP!

▼ Most fishes don't see the eyes and mouth of a stargazer fish from the Red Sea until it's too late. Fishes that hide in the sand can avoid enemies and pounce on their prey without warning.

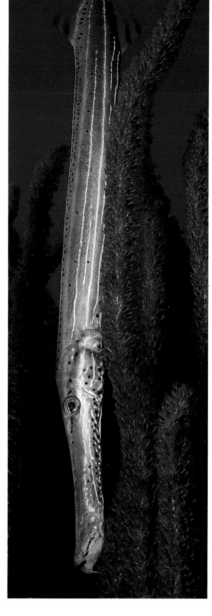

▲ Wrapping its tail around a branch of soft coral, the longsnout sea horse can hold itself still and feed on small animals that float in the water around it.

▶ Alarmed by an intruder, a trumpetfish swims into an upside-down position to blend in well with its surroundings.

Some fishes, like sea horses or trumpetfish, swim or hover straight up and down in the water until a meal comes by. These fishes use their fins and an organ called a "swim bladder" to hold themselves motionless in the water. A swim bladder is like a balloon inside the fish. When the fish needs to float higher in the water, it pumps up its swim bladder with more gas or air. When it wants to sink, it lets the air out again. When a sea horse hovers among water plants, it is almost invisible because it can stay absolutely still and often matches the shapes and colors of its surroundings. A trumpetfish can disappear among branches of soft coral in the same way.

A fish swims by moving its tail and fins. The fins on the top and bottom of a fish's body help it stay upright in the water as it swims. The paired fins help a fish stop, start, and change direction. The tail fin pushes a fish forward as it bends its body from side to side. A few fish that live on the bottom, such as rays, flap their broad fins up and down. Some bottom-dwellers, such as the pancake batfish, even crawl on the fins on their bellies.

▼ A head-on view of the queen angelfish from the Caribbean Sea is a good way to understand how a fish uses its fins. The paired fins set back along both sides of its mouth and on its belly help the fish to steer and maneuver. The tail fin of most fishes helps to propel the fish through the water. The fins on its back help to stabilize the fish in much the same way as a boat's keel.

▲ Faced with so many silvery minnows to choose from, the yellowtail snapper (left) may get confused and let a possible meal swim away. Fishes that swim in schools are better able to find food and escape from other hungry fishes.

Some fishes travel in large groups or schools. A group of large fish may be following—and eating—a school of smaller fish, or gathering around another good source of food.

Fishes traveling in schools sometimes confuse animals that want to eat them. With so many fish in a group, it is hard for a hungry predator to know where to bite first. Traveling in a school also helps members of the group locate food, find mates, and warn each other of danger.

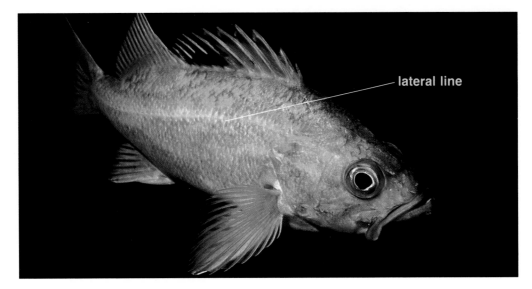

lateral line

▲ The tube or canal called the lateral line runs from the fish's gill cover to its tail. On the canary rockfish, the lateral line is visible as a distinct line outlined in white.

Schooling fishes watch each other to help keep the group together. Each fish can look forward with one eye while the other one is looking backward. Fishes also have another special sense that lets group members know how far apart they are or whether the group is changing direction. On both sides of its body, each fish has a row of pores—or tiny holes in its skin—called the lateral line. Tiny hairs inside the pores are so sensitive that they can feel the slightest ripple or movement in the water. This warning system lets the fish know when another fish or another animal is nearby.

Fishes have several ways of telling what is going on around them in the water. They can see, hear, smell, touch, and taste, just as we can. Their eyesight is quite good, but it is not very useful in deep or murky water. It is easy to hear sounds under water, so fishes often rely more on what they can hear than on what they can see. A fish has no ears on the outside of its body, but it can still pick up sounds well. Most of the sounds a fish hears are the low-pitched grunts, booms, croaks, and clicks that other fishes make.

Sharks are well-known for being able to detect the movements of a struggling fish that could become a meal. They can also smell blood a quarter of a mile (about .4 km) away. Eels also have a very good sense of smell. Some eels even have nostrils on long stalks. This separates and improves their sense of smell since one stalk brings water in and the other sends water out.

Fishes that live in muddy water or hunt for food along the bottom of oceans, rivers, streams, and lakes sometimes have fleshy whiskers called barbels. Catfish use the barbels dangling from their lips to taste the mud and water. Together with its nostrils, the barbels tell the catfish when it has found a worm or something else good to eat.

◄ With its nostrils perched on stalks, a conger eel from the Red Sea is better able to pick up smells of the animals around it. Water goes in one nostril and out the other.

◄ The whiskers of this catfish help it to feel its way around for food in river-bottom mud.

▲ The flightless cormorant bird from the Galápagos Islands hunts underwater to prey on fishes for short periods at a time. Unlike fishes, cormorants need to come to the surface to breathe air.

Other animals besides fishes live or swim in the same kinds of waters. What makes these animals different from fishes?

Many birds, for example, or other animals that live near the shores of fresh or salt water depend on ponds, streams, or bays for food or places to nest. But these animals breathe air and cannot spend their whole lives in the water the way a fish can.

Other animals that spend more time in the water still need to breathe air. They come ashore or to the surface for short times to breathe, and for longer times to rest or raise their families. Turtles, for example, swim in ponds, rivers, or oceans, but crawl onto land to lay their eggs. Frogs spend their early lives as tadpoles, swimming and feeding in water. When they grow up, they develop legs and can hop on land.

▼ Many animals which are not fishes spend part of their lives in water. The glass frog, for example, lays a mass of eggs on the blade of a leaf above a pond or a stream. Once the eggs have hatched into tadpoles, they fall off into the water, where they grow up to be frogs.

A fish does not breathe air the way we and other land animals do. It can live under water safely for its entire life, unless another animal eats it or someone catches it. Whether a fish travels for miles along a coast or only a short distance up- or downstream, it does not need to come up for air.

When we breathe, our lungs take in oxygen from the air. A fish's body is designed to take oxygen directly from the water. As a fish swims, it takes in water through its mouth. Then the water flows over the gills or is pumped back out over them. A fish's gills look red because its blood flows very close to the surface. As water passes over the gills, the fish's blood absorbs oxygen.

Gills are so important to a fish that they need to be protected from bumps and bites. In most fishes, the gills are protected by a bony flap called the gill cover. In sharks or rays, the gills are tucked underneath very tough skin. The gill openings are narrow slits.

Humans and other animals that live on land cannot breathe under water. Instead, we breathe air through our nostrils or mouth. The air passes into our lungs, where oxygen is absorbed into our blood. A fish has nostrils, too, but its nostrils are used for smelling, not for breathing.

▼ ▶ The gills of a fish are noticeably red because the blood flows very close to the gills' surface. When a fish breathes, water passes over its gills, and the water's oxygen is absorbed into the fish's bloodstream. An outer flap of bone surrounds the gills and protects them. Facing page: A close-up of the gills of a salmon.

gills

▲ Whales are mammals, just as we are. We get oxygen from the air through lungs, not gills. The right whale's spout is the breath that's being exhaled as it comes to the surface of the ocean to breathe.

Although they live in the ocean, whales and seals cannot breathe under water. They are mammals, just as we are. Like other mammals—such as cows, horses, dogs, cats, and sheep—they have lungs instead of gills. All whales and seals are wonderful swimmers and divers. They can stay under water for a long time, but sooner or later they must come up to refill their lungs with air.

A whale can be spotted at a distance by its spout. The spout is a cloud of mist that forms as the whale breathes out warm air when it returns to the surface. Most whales breathe through blowholes on the top of their heads.

Seals, sea lions, and walruses breathe through their nostrils. These animals must poke their noses above water to breathe. Harbor seals are very good divers—they can stay under water for up to twenty minutes.

Baby seals are born on land or floating ice, but baby whales are born under water. A baby whale must reach the surface quickly in order to take its first breath of air or it will drown. The baby whale will then return to the surface on its own as it swims and dives with its mother.

Whales and seals spend months caring for their young. The babies nurse on their mother's rich milk until they are ready to catch their own food. Drinking milk and breathing air are two reasons why these animals are more closely related to us than to fishes, even though they live in the water.

▼ Sea lions hunt for food in the water, but give birth on land and breathe air through their lungs.

Newborn fishes usually do not get much help from their parents. Most kinds of fishes just lay their eggs and swim away. A few kinds of fishes make nests on the bottom of a stream or bay. Some fishes even guard their eggs or young. A few kinds of fishes carry their eggs in their mouths to keep them safe. Other young fishes may be eaten by their parents.

Some fishes may pick up their young in their mouths to move them away from danger. A female seahorse places her eggs inside the male's special fold of skin or pouch, which is somewhat like a kangaroo's. The eggs develop there until they are released into the water.

The eggs of some fishes drift away on the water currents. Other fishes' eggs sink to the bottom or stick to water plants. Sometimes people keep boats in places that are also nurseries for baby fishes. When people dig up or scrape away the bottom of a harbor or river to make a deeper or wider channel for boats, the eggs of fishes and other water animals may be scraped away at the same time. If the eggs and water plants are taken away, the young animals will not hatch.

Most fishes hatch from eggs, but some grow inside their mothers. A baby shark develops inside its mother and looks like its parents—it is just smaller. Many young fishes, such as damselfish and wrasses, do not look much like their parents. Their colors and patterns change as they become old enough to attract mates.

One female fish may lay thousands, even millions, of eggs. Many young fishes will hatch and survive. Many will be eaten by other animals, including other fishes

▶ An ocean fish called a cabezon lays many hundreds of eggs in a mass glued to a surface like a rock. The male fish shown here guards the developing young until they hatch. Inset: Inside each of the transparent egg capsules is a nearly fully developed baby cabezon fish. Once the eggs hatch, the newborn fish are no longer protected by their parents. They are at the mercy of hungry fish in the ocean around them.

A young fish must survive other dangers besides predators. The water where it lives may become too warm or too cold. There may not be enough food for it to eat. If the water is too dirty or polluted, young fishes will not grow up to be bigger fishes. People can help young fishes survive by taking good care of the waters where fishes hatch and feed.

The water is home to other animals besides fishes. There are some other animals that can spend their entire lives under water. Like fishes, they can swim, find and catch food, raise their young, and avoid danger in the water. They can even breathe under water in the same way that fishes can. However, unlike fishes, these animals, which are called invertebrates, do not have a backbone.

▼ Trash and chemicals thrown into rivers, oceans, and streams can poison the water and destroy nurseries for baby fishes and other water animals.

▲ The rock crab, shown here eating a sea slug, spends its life living and breathing underwater. Why isn't it an example of a fish?

If you have ever seen someone clean a fish after he or she has caught it, you know that a fish has a backbone. So does a seal, a whale, a beaver, a turtle, a bird, a snake, and a frog. We have a backbone, too. Backbones and other bones attached to them support our bodies and help us move. These bones also help to protect the heart, lungs, stomach, and other important parts inside our bodies.

Fishes are the largest group of animals with backbones alive today. Water animals without backbones are not fishes. A crab, unlike a fish, does not have a backbone. Its body is protected by a hard shell. As the crab grows, it will shed its shell and grow a new one that fits its body.

Each kind of fish is as important as the next. If we don't protect fishes in the places where they live, some fishes will be lost forever. Here are some things you can do to help. Make sure no one in your community or home town dumps sewage, oil, or harmful chemicals into the water or the ground nearby. When you go fishing, let the little catch go—it is against the law to keep fish that are too small. Some fishes should not be caught at all. Try not to catch more fish than you need. Save some for tomorrow. If too many fish are taken from the same place year after year, they may disappear for good.

Each kind of fish is important for the role it plays in the water world. Two-thirds of our planet is covered with water. By taking good care of fishes and their homes, we can help make the earth a better place for all of us to live.

▼ **The future of the rainbow trout, a popular sport fish, depends on protecting the rivers and streams that provide it with a home. Trout thrive in cool, unpolluted waters which contain lots of oxygen.**

On the next few pages, you will see several animals that live in or near the water. Use these clues to help you figure out whether each animal is a fish: Does it have fins? Does it have a backbone? Can it breathe under water? Does it have to come up for air? How does it swim or float?

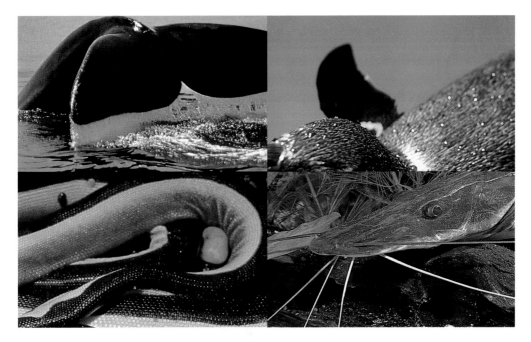

TAILS AND SCALES

The animal you see in the picture below (left) is an eel. It looks like a snake, but it lives in the water. Is it a fish? Where are its fins? How does it swim? Does it have to come up for air? What makes an eel different from a snake?

An eel is a fish. It breathes under water and has round gill openings. As is true of water snakes, most eels swim by slithering through the water. But unlike snakes, eels do not have to come up for air. Snakes do not have gills. They breathe air, as we do. They cannot breathe under water. A water snake often pokes its head above water to breathe as it swims. It lays its eggs on land, not in the water.

As we have seen with other snakes, water snakes are covered with scales. Even their eyes are covered by scales. Unlike most fishes, eels do not seem to have scales. But the scales are so tiny that you cannot see them. A snake sheds its skin when it outgrows it. Eels do not shed their skin. Their skin is covered with slime. Snakes are not slimy. Their skin is smooth but dry.

Most eels have a pair of fins on each side of their body, just behind the head. Some eels also have a long ridge of fins along the top and bottom of their body. These fins merge with the tail, which tapers to a point. In moray eels, the skin is so thick that it covers the fins.

▼ Although this eel (left) looks like a snake, it is actually a fish. It gets oxygen from the water with gills just as other fishes do.
▼ Sea snakes (right) don't have gills and cannot breathe underwater. They lay their eggs on land.

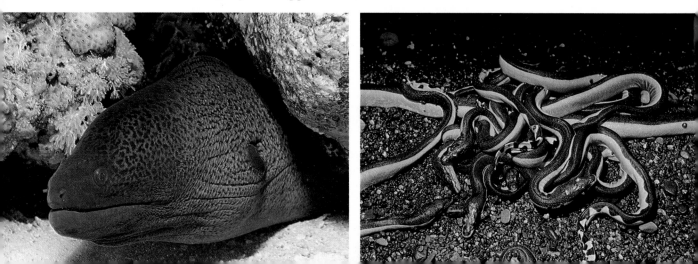

FINS, FLIPPERS, AND FLUKES

When you see a fin sticking above the waves, how can you tell whether it belongs to a shark or a whale? Is it a fish or a mammal?

If you see a group of finned creatures arching their backs as they leap above the waves, you are probably watching a group of dolphins. Dolphins are whales. Dolphins are mammals, not fish.

Whales have horizontal tails called flukes. They flip their flukes up and down, not side to side, as they push themselves forward in the water with their flukes and flippers.

A shark is a fish. Most sharks bend their bodies from side to side as they swim. They propel themselves with their fins and tails. A shark's tail is vertical—upright—in the water. It knifes through the water in the same way the fins on a shark's back do as it swims. The shark has gill slits instead of a blowhole. Like other fishes, sharks do not have to come up for air—they can stay under water for as long as they live.

A killer whale has a high fin on its back that may remind you of a shark's fin. But as is true of other whales, it is a mammal, not a fish.

▼ Whales are mammals, not fishes. They use a horizontal tail with a pair of flattened flukes to push themselves forward through the water.

WINGS AND WEBBED FEET

Are animals with wings and webbed feet that live in or near the water fishes? In the picture below (left), the animal held by its fins is a fish, not a bird. It is called a flying fish. In the picture below (right), the animal gliding through the water with its wings spread apart is a bird, not a fish. It is a penguin. Penguins teeter about as they walk on land, but they cannot fly.

Like other birds, penguins lay their eggs on land, not in the water. Penguins do not make fancy nests, but they protect their eggs carefully with their feet. Penguins breathe air, as do other birds.

Flying fish cannot really fly or flap their "wings." In fact, they do not have wings at all. But they can soar through the air for several hundred feet on their long, paired fins. As each flying fish gets ready to take off, it swims faster and faster, pushing its tail from side to side. After a final strong push of its tail, the fish leaps out of the water with its fins spread out to the side, like wings. Flying fish usually take off to avoid their enemies or a boat that has startled them, but they sometimes "fly" for other reasons. Like other fishes, they live in the water and breathe through gills.

▼ The fins of a flying fish act like wings to help it soar above the surface of the water.

▼ Penguins do their flying under water, using flippers to help them maneuver.

WHISKERS AND FUR

A catfish or sea lion can use its whiskers to feel its way around in the water, just as we can use our fingertips to feel our way along a wall in the dark. Nurse sharks, which feed on crabs and shellfish on the bottom of the ocean, also have fleshy whiskers. Nurse sharks rest on the bottom of the ocean when they get tired.

Nurse sharks and catfishes are fishes, with fins and gills. Although one kind of catfish can "walk" across land for short distances when its watery home dries up, most fishes cannot survive for very long on land.

A sea lion can haul itself out of the water and hop along on its flippers on the beach or lie down to rest or nurse its young. It is a mammal, not a fish. It breathes air and has lungs instead of gills. Another big difference is that the sea lion is covered with sleek fur and has a layer of fat under its skin to help it keep warm. Like other mammals, including people, the sea lion needs to keep its body at the same temperature all the time. A fish's body changes temperature with the water around it.

Now you know what makes a fish a fish, so the next time someone asks, "Is it a fish?" you'll know the answer.

▼ There are many animals besides the catfish, shown here, which swim and feel their way around in the water. Can you name some?

GLOSSARY

Backbone (BAK-bone)—a column of bones that gives support to a vertebrate animal's body.

Barbels (BAR-bulls)—fleshy, whiskerlike tentacles near the mouth of some kinds of fish which are used to taste or touch their surroundings.

Blowhole (BLOW HOLE)—a breathing hole (some whales have two holes) on the top of a whale's head through which it breathes in and out.

Coral reef (KOR-ul REEF)—a huge, natural formation made by the abandoned limestone skeletons of coral animals found only in the tropics.

Eel—slimy water animals that look like snakes, but are fish and have gills that remove oxygen from the surrounding water.

Fin—an extended part from the body of a fish or other water animal used mainly to swim, steer, or maintain balance.

Fish vs. fishes—How are these terms used? Use "fish" when referring to one species (ten salmon are ten fish). Use "fishes" when referring to more than one species (ten salmon, three trout, and one codfish are fourteen fishes).

Flipper (FLIP-ur)—a marine mammal's paddlelike wing, which helps the animal to swim.

Fluke (FLEWK)—the tail of dolphins and other whales, which they flex up and down to move them through the water.

Flying fish—certain kinds of fishes, which can use their tails and other fins to jump out of the water and "fly" for short distances, before they fall back into the water.

Freshwater fishes—fishes that live in lakes, rivers, streams, and ponds which contain fresh water, not salt or ocean water.

Gills (GILZ)—feathery organs on both sides of the head or body of fishes and aquatic invertebrates, which absorb oxygen from water and remove carbon dioxide from the blood.

Gill cover—a protective flaplike covering over a fish's gills, which a fish can open and close to let water in and out.

Invertebrate (in-VERT-uh-brate)—an animal without a backbone, such as a jellyfish, lobster, or insect.

Lateral line (LAT-ur-ul LINE)—a system of tiny holes (pores) running along both sides of a fish's body, which enable it to detect movement in the water.

Lung—an organ for breathing oxygen. Most fishes have gills to absorb oxygen from water, although some fishes (lungfish, for example) have a lung to survive in oxygen-poor swamps.

Mammal (MAM-ul)—any of a group of vertebrates, including humans, who have hair and nourish their young with milk from mammary glands.

Nostrils (NOHS-trils)—outside openings along a fish's snout, which enable a fish to detect smells in the surrounding water.

Nursery—In a fish's world, a nursery is a place, such as a salt marsh, where baby fishes can find lots of food and places to hide from other hungry animals.

Plankton (PLANK-tun)—free-floating, often microscopic, plants or animals that live in water and are transported largely by water currents.

Pores—In a fish's lateral line, pores are tiny openings in the skin through which water and water vibrations pass and which allow a fish to sense movement around it.

School—Hundreds, even thousands, of fishes gather in groups to increase protection, and to make it easier to find food and mates. Fish in a school usually swim parallel and close to one another, and they are often the same kind of fish.

Soft corals (SOFT KOR-ulz)—corals such as sea fans and sea plumes with flexible skeletons that can bend in water currents.

Spout (SPOWT)—the exhaled breath of a whale through its blowhole(s) produces a spray that commercial whalers called a "spout" or a "blow."

Swim bladder (SWIM BLAD-ur)—a gas-filled sac beneath a fish's backbone which helps it to rise or sink and, in some fishes, aids in hearing and making sounds; also called the gas or air bladder.

Water snake—a snake that lives in or around the water but which cannot breathe underwater. Water snakes lay eggs on land and shed their skin just as land snakes do.

FOR FURTHER READING

Allen, Gertrude. *Everyday Turtles, Toads, and Their Kin.* Boston: Houghton Mifflin, 1970.

Bailey, Jill. *Fish.* New York: Facts On File, 1990.

Bunting, Eve. *The Sea World Book of Whales,* A Sea World Book for Young Readers. New York and London: Harcourt Brace Jovanovich, 1980.

Burton, Maurice, and Cole, Joanna. *A Snake's Body.* New York: William Morrow, 1981.

Eastman, David. *Now I Know What Is a Fish.* Mahwah, NJ: Troll Associates, 1982.

Fletcher, Alan Mark. *Fishes That Hide.* Reading, MA: Addison-Wesley, 1973.

Parker, Steve. *Fish: Eyewitness Books.* New York: Alfred A. Knopf, 1990.

―――. *Pond and River: Eyewitness Books.* New York: Alfred A. Knopf, 1988.

Patent, Dorothy Hinshaw. *Dolphins and Porpoises.* New York: Holiday House, 1987.

―――. *Fish and How They Reproduce.* New York: Holiday House, 1976.

Quinn, Kay. *A Look at Fish.* Los Angeles: Price Stern Sloan, 1986.

Ranger Rick. *Amazing Creatures of the Sea.* Washington: National Wildlife Federation, 1987.

Sabin, Louis. *Fish.* Mahwah, NJ: Troll Associates, 1984.

Segaloff, Nat and Erickson, Paul. Illustrated by Bob Barner. *Fish Tales.* New York: Sterling Publishing Company, 1990.

Tayntor, Liz, Erickson, Paul, and Kaufman, Les. *Dive to the Coral Reefs.* New York: Crown Publishers, 1986.

Todd, Frank S. *The Sea World Book of Penguins,* A Sea World Book for Young Readers. New York and London: Harcourt Brace Jovanovich, 1981.

Wheeler, Alwyne. *Discovering Saltwater Fish.* New York: Franklin Watts, 1988.

INDEX

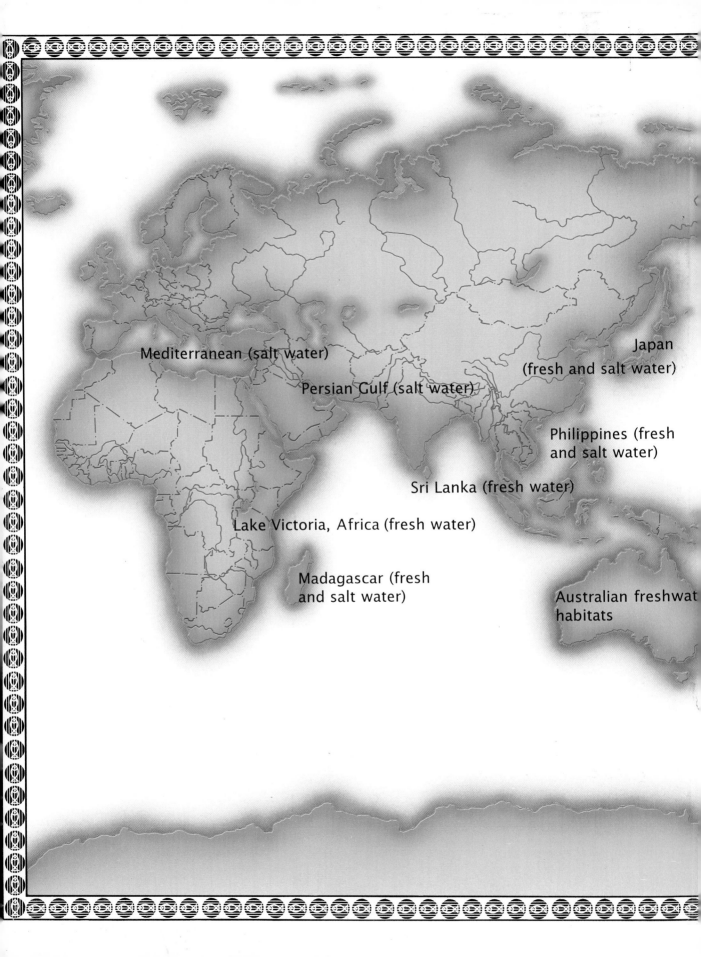

Mediterranean (salt water)

Japan
(fresh and salt water)

Persian Gulf (salt water)

Philippines (fresh
and salt water)

Sri Lanka (fresh water)

Lake Victoria, Africa (fresh water)

Madagascar (fresh
and salt water)

Australian freshwat
habitats